W9-AHY-584

Editor: Penny Clarke
Consultant: Jacqueline Morley

Produced by
THE SALARIYA BOOK CO. LTD
25 Marlborough Place
Brighton BN1 1UB
United Kingdom

© The Salariya Book Co. Ltd MCMXCVII

First published in 1997 by
Franklin Watts
96 Leonard Street
London EC2A 4RH

First American edition 1998 by
Franklin Watts
A Division of Grolier Publishing
Sherman Turnpike
Danbury, CT 06816

ISBN 0 -531-14466-6

Library of Congress Cataloging-in-Publication Data
Steedman, Scott
 Egyptian Town / written by Scott Steedman ;
 illustrated by David Antram ; created and
designed by David Salariya.
    p. cm -- (Metropolis)
 Includes index.
 Summary: Takes the reader through a typical town in ancient Egypt around 1200 B.C.,
 visiting the different areas, major buildings, and describing how the people lived.
 ISBN 0-531-14466-6
  1. Egypt--Civilization--To 332 B.C.--Juvenile literature.
2. Cities and towns, Ancient--Egypt--Juvenile literature.
[1. Egypt--Civilization--To 332 B.C. 2. Cities and towns, Ancient.]
I. Salariya, David. II. Antram, David, 1958- ill. III. Title.
IV. Series: Metropolis (New York, N.Y.)
DT61.S8654   1998
932--dc21   97-2844
                              CIP AC

Printed in Singapore.

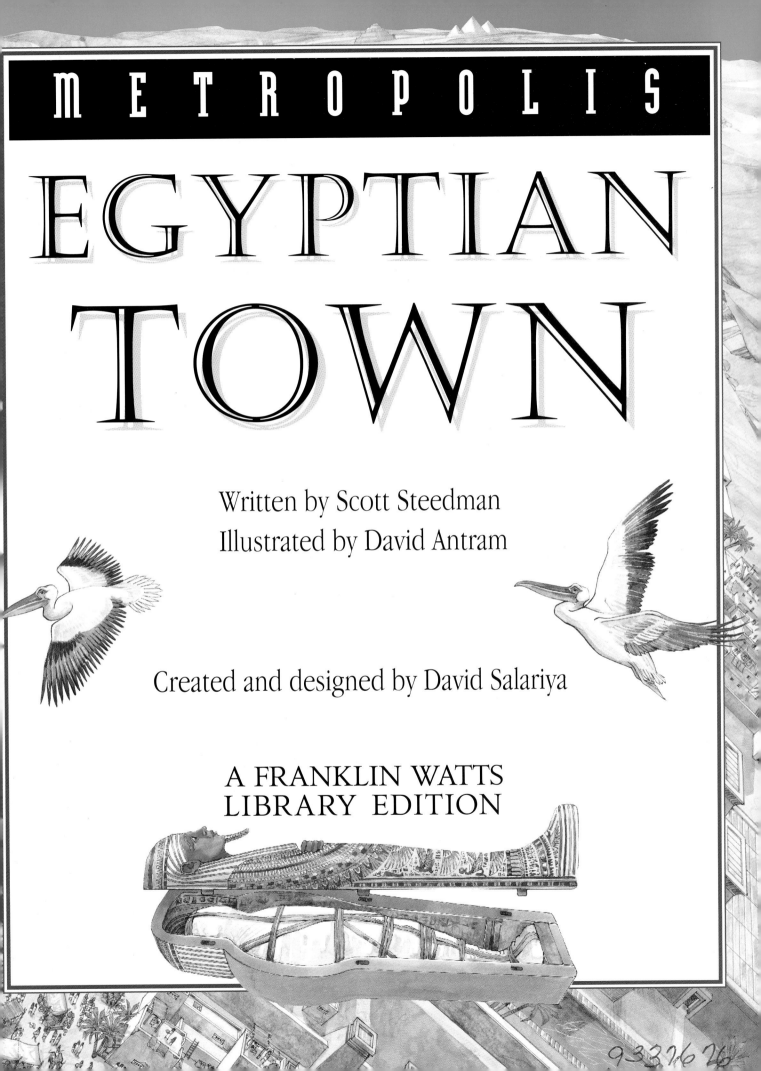

METROPOLIS

EGYPTIAN TOWN

Written by Scott Steedman

Illustrated by David Antram

Created and designed by David Salariya

A FRANKLIN WATTS
LIBRARY EDITION

93376 26

Contents

INTRODUCTION

Over 5,000 years ago, the Egyptians created the world's first great civilization by the Nile River. For the next twenty-five centuries it was the richest and most powerful civilization in the world. Historians usually divide this huge stretch of time into three periods, called kingdoms. The first pharaoh – the Egyptian word for king – united the country around 3000 BC. At the same time hieroglyphs, one of the first forms of picture writing, were perfected. The great pyramids were built in the period that followed, the Old Kingdom (2686–2181 BC). During the Middle Kingdom (2133–1786 BC) strong pharaohs expanded the empire. Art, especially the carving of magnificent life-size stone statues, flourished. The New Kingdom (1567–1085 BC), was Egypt's golden age. Mighty pharaohs such as Amenhotep III and Ramses the Great built massive temples, and were buried in spectacular tombs together with priceless treasures.

This book is about a New Kingdom town in around 1200 BC. It is not the capital, just an everyday city. Its wealth can be seen in the pharaoh's palace and the great temple. But like every town, it has poor districts where servants and craftsmen live cramped together. Merchants and government officials arrive by boat and hurry through the narrow streets. And in the fields by the river, farmers work the soil just as their families have done for centuries.

AROUND THE TOWN

Workers' houses
Ordinary workers live in tiny mud-brick apartments, built one upon the other. They share the small smoky rooms with children, grandparents, cats, and even pet monkeys.

Mummification
Dead Egyptians are turned into mummies in the embalming tents. This sacred work is performed by priests from the nearby temple.

Farms and fields
The green fields by the river are ideal for growing wheat, barley, and flax. The farmers, whose homes are simple mud-brick houses, also rear cattle and geese and tend their vegetable gardens.

River traffic
People, messages, and goods all travel by river. Boats, powered either by oars or sails, bring travelers, fishermen, or merchants from faraway lands. These men are hunting a hippopotamus.

Nobleman's villa
Some members of the royal family live in the palace. Others have villas in quiet locations, with shady gardens and well-stocked fish ponds.

Valley of the Kings
For centuries, Egypt's greatest pharaohs have been buried in this desolate spot. It is guarded day and night, and visits are strictly forbidden.

Mortuary temple
To pay respects to a dead king or relative, Egyptians visit the mortuary temple. They recite prayers and leave offerings of food and wine.

Pharaoh's palace
This is just one of the pharaoh's many houses. When he visits the town, he stays here with his many wives and servants. Princes, princesses, and officials live here all year round.

Temple
The biggest and most impressive building in town is the temple, home to priests, scribes (professional writers), and officials. It includes craft workshops, storehouses, and kitchens.

Market
There are very few shops, and most goods are bought and sold in the crowded market, right by the pier.

Harbor
All day long, goods such as wheat, wine, building stone, horses, and dried fish are loaded and unloaded in the bustling harbor.

Merchants' houses
Rich merchants live in luxurious town houses near the quay. These have large rooms for the family, and smaller ones for the servants.

11

FISHING IN THE RIVER

The marshes by the Nile River teem with fish and flocks of ducks, long-legged cranes, and other birds. Rich Egyptians love fishing and hunting birds. These exciting sports are ways of proving their skill and courage. Ordinary people fish and hunt, too, but for meat rather than sport. Like most things the Egyptians do, fishing and hunting also have a religious meaning. The hippopotamus, for instance, is a dangerous animal that kills hundreds of people every year. In Egyptian legend it is a symbol of the evil god Seth. Hunters risk their lives spearing hippopotamuses from flimsy rafts. By killing one, they score a victory for good, and help to restore order to the world.

Egyptian hunters use hooks and harpoon tips made of copper or bronze. Hooks are used for angling – fishing with a line. Rich Egyptians often do this in the well-stocked pools in their gardens.

A nobleman sees a flock of ducks. His wife and daughter steady the raft as he takes aim.

The nobleman knocks the birds down with a heavy throwing stick, a special hunting weapon. Sometimes the pet cat is sent to fetch the injured birds.

Standing on their raft made of bundles of papyrus reeds, fishermen drag nets (also made from reeds) through the water. They keep an eye out for Nile crocodiles, which can grow to twenty-two feet (eight meters) long.

As one hunter spears a hippopotamus, a second keeps the raft clear of the angry giant. A third man pulls ropes attached to the harpoon tip, which stays in the animal's back.

To catch live birds, hunters set traps with nets. They break the birds' wings, then take them away in cages.

THE FARMING YEAR

Akhet, the time of flood, lasts from July until October by today's calendar.

Peret, the time to plant the fields, is between November and February.

Shemu, the period when crops are harvested, lasts from March to June.

Every year, the local tax scribe visits the farm. He asks the farmer how much wheat and flax he has planted and how many fruit trees or vines he has. If the farmer keeps cows or geese, the scribe counts them and writes down how many there are.

Cattle farmers drink the milk from their cows, and also make it into butter and cheese.

Most ancient Egyptians are farmers whose lives follow the rhythms of the Nile River. It rains little in Egypt and is hot all year round. But in late spring every year the Nile floods its banks and brings water to the fields. This is Akhet, the time of flood. It is a season of rest, when farmers repair tools or drink beer in the shade. It is followed by Peret, when the waters fall, leaving fertile black soil on the fields. This is the time to plow the fields, sow crops, and build new irrigation channels. Next comes Shemu, the time of harvest, when everybody works hard to bring in the crops before the Nile rises again.

Meat is a luxury and is only eaten on special occasions.

The scribe works out how much tax the farmer owes. The farmer pays it in wheat or cattle. Anyone caught cheating is beaten.

Grapes are grown for eating and to make wine. Farm workers squeeze the juice out with their bare feet. Then it is left to age in clay jars. Each jar is marked with the year and the name of the farm.

Farmers train baboon monkeys to pick figs from branches high up in the trees.

CRAFTWORKERS

Next to the town's temple is a large workshop complex where skilled craftworkers produce beautiful goods for the priests and temple officials. Sculptors carve statues from stone and wood, potters sweat over their wheels, and jewelers fashion glittering works from gold and gemstones. Carpenters make furniture, chariots, and mummy cases, while glassmakers shape bowls and jars in vivid colors. Elsewhere, painters, metalworkers, and weavers are busy. The workers put in four hours each morning, then have lunch and a nap before working another four-hour shift in the afternoon. The working week is ten days, followed by a rest day.

Craftworkers are men. Girls can marry from the age of 12, so are busy with their children.

Craftsmen often make wooden toys in their spare time.

The workshop also has a big kitchen where cooks bake bread, brew beer, butcher animals, and prepare meals. Workers are always paid in wheat, vegetables, fish, wine, or wood for fuel, according to what is available.

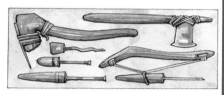

The Egyptians have not discovered iron, so their hardest tools have blades of copper or bronze, which need regular straightening or replacing. Tools are valuable and the foremen count them carefully out and back each day.

Only the rich store household goods in chests. Most people use baskets (below) made from coils of palm leaves, cane, or papyrus.

Two metalworkers (above) hold a pot of metal over a fire. Another stokes the flames of the fire with a pair of foot-powered bellows.

The liquid metal is poured into molds.

The workshop foreman is a scribe. He checks all the finished work, and weighs valuable items like jewelery to make sure that no one has stolen any of the gold.

PYRAMIDS AND TOMBS

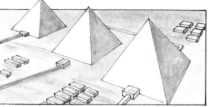

The first Egyptian pharaohs (kings) were buried in pyramids. The pyramids at Giza are the largest. It took thousands of men many years to build these huge tombs. Robbers stole the treasures buried in them long ago.

The Egyptians build their tombs on the west bank of the Nile. This is the Land of the Dead, where the sun god Amun-Ra sets over the desert every evening. The Sun's journey inspires the Egyptians. After death, they believe that a person's spirit travels through the underworld, like the sun at night. If it survives the dangerous journey, the spirit rises again, like the sun in the morning. To prepare for the next world, rich Egyptians are buried with clothing, tools, furniture, make-up, games, even loaves of bread, and fine wines. Their magnificent tombs are cut deep into the rock. The walls are painted with magic spells and pictures of the gods, to help them on their way.

The Book of the Dead, a painted papyrus scroll, has spells for life in the underworld.

Egyptian artists' materials.

The tombs of kings, queens, and wealthy officials are decorated with wall paintings. Teams of artists work all year round decorating the tombs. A skilled draftsman draws up a grid, then sketches out the design. Sometimes he copies this from a pattern book, perhaps adapting it to suit the individual tomb. Painters mix bright colors from ground-up rocks and charcoal, then paint over the sketch using reed brushes.

PREPARING A MUMMY

To live forever, an Egyptian must preserve his or her body for the next world. This process is called mummification. It is carried out in tents on the Nile's east bank by special priests known as embalmers, and takes eighty days. The priests bless every stage of the process, chanting spells, burning incense, and sprinkling the dead body with sacred water. Early in Egypt's history, only kings and queens were mummified. But now everyone who can afford it has their body preserved. Mummy-making has become an industry, and you can buy all the accessories in a range of styles to suit your tastes and budget.

Canopic jars decorated with the heads of gods, called the Sons of Horus, hold the dead person's organs.

Sacred animals and pets, such as cats, dogs, snakes, crocodiles, and even dung beetles (a symbol of the sun), are mummified.

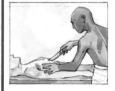

The embalmers wash the body with palm wine. Then they cut it open with a sacred knife.

.They remove the liver, lungs, stomach, and intestines, and put them in the special canopic jars.

They hook the brain out through the nose, then cover the body in salt and leave it to dry out.

Forty days later, the priests begin to wrap the body in roll after roll of tight linen bandages.

They replace lost limbs with fake ones, and put magic amulets between the bandages.

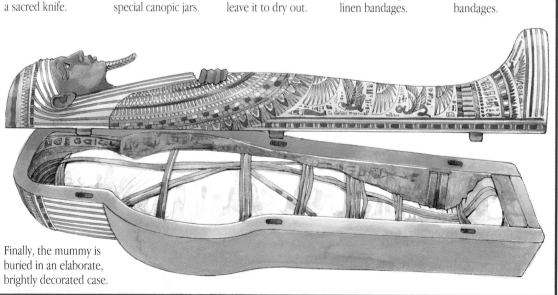

Finally, the mummy is buried in an elaborate, brightly decorated case.

A MORTUARY TEMPLE

The pharaoh, Egypt's beloved god-king, has died. His body has been mummified, and now it is time for him to travel to the Land of the Dead, where he will rejoin the gods. The day of the funeral is a national holiday, and people come from far away by boat or on foot. Huge crowds watch in awe as priests steer the pharaoh's body across the Nile and carry it to the mortuary temple. Here priests conduct the last rites before burying the king in a secret tomb. For years to come, the temple priests will make offerings of food to the spirit of the dead pharaoh who is now a god.

Women are hired to cry, wail, throw earth in the air, and chant funeral songs along the route of the procession.

Priests and relatives of the dead person will take food to the mortuary temple. It is the duty of the living to ensure that the spirit of their dead relative has enough to eat.

The most important ceremony at the funeral is the Opening of the Mouth. This is meant to give the dead king back his senses, so he will be able to speak and eat in the next world.

Priests chant holy words and carry the king's treasure to the temple where he is to be buried.

Prayers and offerings are made to slabs of wood painted with spells and pictures of the gods.

The Pharaoh's Palace

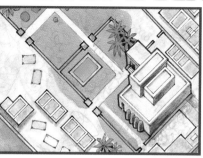

The pharaoh lives in a sumptuous palace by the Nile. The Egyptians believe he is the son of the sun god Amun-Ra, sent to earth to protect Egypt and its people. His power is awesome. He judges criminals and leads the army in battle. Everyone in the palace dedicates their lives to pleasing this living god. He has hundreds of servants to wash and dress him and answer his every desire. Others fan him, cook his meals, and look after his horses. On holidays, they carry him through the streets as the people cheer. Musicians and dancing girls perform for him, and wrestlers fight for his pleasure.

The pharaoh wears a crown and the royal false beard. He holds the crook and flail, symbols of rebirth. They are associated with the ancient king Osiris who, according to legend, was the first pharaoh to be reborn after death.

In theory, the pharaoh rules the country by himself. In reality, he is surrounded by officials who advise him. They have titles like "Overseer of the Granaries" and "Fanbearer on the Right of the King."

Most men only have one wife. But a pharaoh can have twenty or thirty, with one special favorite. Relations between the wives and their many children can be extremely difficult.

AT THE TEMPLE

The town's temple is dedicated to one of Egypt's many gods. The Egyptians regard it as the god's house. Only priests are allowed to enter the sacred inner rooms. At the heart of the complex stands a golden shrine containing a statue of the god. Every morning, as the first rays of sunlight enter the room, the priests open the shrine. Burning incense and reciting prayers, they dress the statue and place a meal before it. This process is repeated several times a day. The temple has its own workshops, kitchens, and farms where the food for offerings is produced.

The priests burn incense (a special gum) in the temple to please the god with its sweet smell.

Priests are called "servants of the gods". To show their purity they wash and shave their heads and bodies regularly. Priests who serve the god Amun-Ra wear leopard-skin robes.

Pylon gateway

Courtyard

Columns

Hypostyle hall

Shrine

Inner rooms

Scribe schools, where boys learn to write, are part of the temple complex.

In the New Kingdom period (1567–1085 BC), Amun-Ra was the chief god.

Inside the temple's great gateway is a courtyard which leads to a hypostyle hall. This has rows of elegant columns shaped and painted like lotuses or papyrus buds. (The lotus is a sacred plant.) Beyond the hall are the sacred inner rooms.

The incense used in temple ceremonies has to be imported and is expensive. But the holy water comes from the temple's own sacred lake.

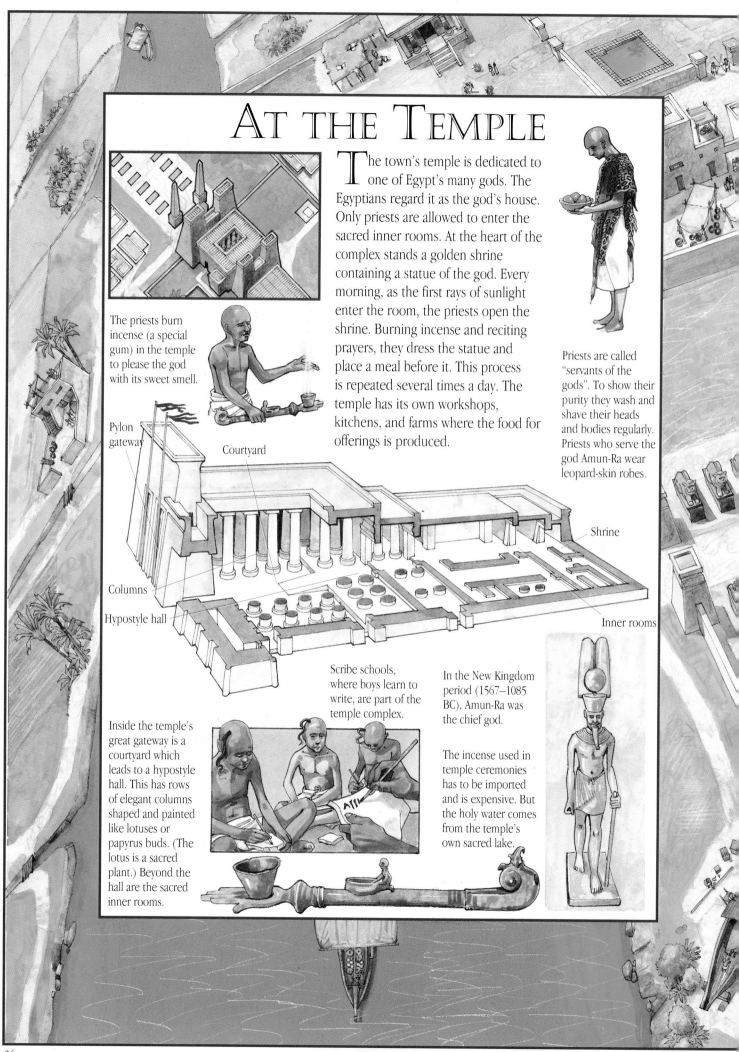

THE QUAYSIDE

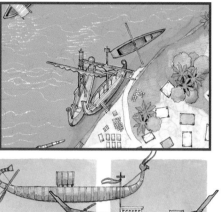

Trade and transportation center on the Nile. Egypt has few roads because they are hard to build on the shifting desert sands. The great river is the country's only highway, linking every important town, temple, and tomb. When the pharaoh visits a town, he arrives in his spectacular royal barge. An ancient text says: "Merchants sail upstream and downstream, eager to convey goods from one place to another and to supply whatever is needed anywhere." Seagoing trading ships jostle with pleasure boats and fishermen's rafts for a place at the quayside. All day long, linen, dried fish, wine, wheat, horses, and building stone are loaded and unloaded.

Boat from before 3100 BC (above left). Made of bundles of papyrus reeds, it is steered with two large oars.

Royal barge of 3000 BC (above right). The first pharaohs stood on the bow of a wooden ship like this when they toured their kingdom.

Cargo ship of about 1300 BC. Although slow, boats like this can carry big loads up and down the Nile. But they are too shallow to brave the open ocean.

Sea-going ship, after 2700 BC. It is flexible and fairly narrow, so it is able to sail on rough seas.

Pilgrimage barge (about 2500 BC). Made of wood and papyrus, it has a canopy for shade.

Transport ship, 2200 BC. Slow but roomy, it has a flat bottom for crossing the Nile's sandbanks.

Pharaoh's barge, 2550 BC (back), has 12 oarsmen and a mast but no sail.

A pleasure boat of 2000 BC. Its mast is only used for sailing upstream when the wind is behind it.

The Egyptians import many luxury goods from Punt, on the coast of east Africa. Traders brave the wild Indian Ocean to get there. Here they load their ships with gold, ebony, incense trees, exotic oils and resins, ivory, leopard skins, pet dogs, and baboons.

THE MARKET-PLACE

On market days, the whole town heads for the large open space by the quayside. Farmers from miles around come by boat to sell their cattle, ducks, and other produce. Families stock up with wheat or barley, to bake bread and brew beer, and linen for making clothes. Wine-growers from the delta haggle over wine, sold in amphorae (tall clay pots). Pet cats, honey, and luxuries such as walnuts, plums, and watermelons are all on sale. Foreign traders attract crowds. The Nubians sell ostriches, giraffes' tails, ebony, and ivory from the south. The Palestinians have horses, silver, and fine cedar wood to sell.

How much is that? Egyptians have no money. An item is weighed, then traded for another item, or items, of equal value.

Traders use copper weights, in units called *debens* (about 91 grams).

Common foods include fish, figs, pomegranates, eggs, leeks, lettuce, dates, garlic, onions, grapes, and honey.

The Egyptians brew their own beer from wheat or barley. They drink it through a straw or hollow reed to filter out the lumps.

Beer and bread are staples of the Egyptians' diet. In this model from a tomb men brew beer in tall tubs and women grind corn.

Slaves are unusual in Egypt. But all wealthy households have servants who help with the shopping and cooking.

Rather than fill the house with smoke, poor Egyptians cook outdoors, roasting fish and birds, and meat on special occasions, over charcoal in a small open brazier.

A MERCHANT'S HOUSE

A rich merchant or official has a house in the center of town, close to the quayside, the temple, and the palace. He may also have a country villa, where he can hunt or relax by the garden pool in the hot summer months. The town house, built of mud bricks like most Egyptian buildings, has three main floors. The ground floor is the servants' quarters. On the first floor are the reception rooms and family bedrooms. These have high ceilings, supported by walls and columns painted with bright plant and animal designs. Upstairs is an office, as well as guest-rooms and storerooms. The roof is used for cooking. It is also the coolest place to relax on hot evenings.

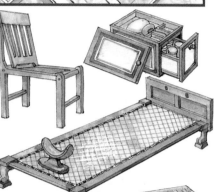

Furniture is very simple. Stools are common, but chairs are rare. Beds are low and long.

The best cups and jars are made of faience pottery, glazed with brightly colored patterns.

Wealthier Egyptians wear clothes of linen which is made from the fibers of the flax plant.

After it is harvested (top), the flax stalks are beaten (above) and the heads are taken off the fibers.

Next, the plant's fine fibers are combed out and spun together to form long threads.

The thread is woven into linen cloth on a loom. Both men and women work as weavers.

This is the house of Djehuty-nefer, a wealthy official. He paid a craftsman to paint this picture of his home in Thebes on the wall of his tomb.

A Nobleman's Feast

A member of the royal family has invited all his friends to a feast at his country house. As the host and hostess greet their guests, servants hand them garlands of flowers to put around their necks, and perfumed wax cones to put on their wigs. The guests sit on stools or cushions at small tables and servants bring them wine and rich food. The host and two important guests sit on elegant wooden chairs. Musicians play during the meal. After the plates have been cleared away, dancing girls wearing nothing but tiny skirts perform acrobatic routines. The wine flows endlessly. Any guests who drink too much can ask a servant to bring them a bowl so they can be sick.

Professional dancers and acrobats live in the pharaoh's palace. They perform at feasts, festivals, and marriages. Two women usually dance together. But men never dance with women.

The gardens of nobles and officials are full of different trees to give scent, shade, and fruit. Such gardens are signs of their owners' wealth.

Musicians provide entertainment at every feast. The ancient harper's song says: "Enjoy yourself while you live . . . Be joyful and make merry."

A nobleman's garden would be incomplete without a pool. He and his family can relax by the pool and if anyone feels bored they can try catching. the fish kept in it.

Time-Traveler's Guide

Getting Around

The best way to get to any Egyptian town is by boat. Ferries come and go all the time, so just go down to the harbor and ask about the next sailing. The captain will tell you the cost. Prices vary with demand and the seasons – they are highest during the flood, when the river is treacherous – so be prepared to bargain just before the ship sails. And don't be surprised if your fellow passengers include cattle, horses, or pet baboons!

If you are heading for Libya or the Faiyum Oasis, you can hitch a ride across the desert with a merchant's caravan. You can hire a donkey, or better still a horse (camels have not been introduced to Egypt yet). Make sure to stock up with water before you leave – the desert is a harsh place, and water will cost a lot more in the oases along your route.

In town, most people get around on foot – except the pharaoh, who is carried everywhere in his golden litter. If you are going to do a lot of sightseeing, you could hire a donkey for the week.

What to Wear

Egypt is very hot all year round. In the daytime, the temperature is almost always over 30° Celsius, so dress lightly. Don't be shocked by the nakedness you will see everywhere. The locals are not shy about their bodies – farmers and manual workers wear very few clothes. In town, people dress up more, but no one wears underclothes, so you can often see their bodies through the thin fabric of their clothes.

Most clothes are made of white linen, the thinner the better. Men usually wear simple wrap-around skirts and leave their chests bare, or throw a light cloak over their shoulders. Women wear long, clinging dresses. On formal occasions, both men and women wear longer, more elaborate outfits and lots of make-up, especially the thick black eye paint called *kohl*. If you are invited to an important dinner, ask your hotel (or your host's servants) to press hundreds of tiny pleats into your outfit. And a wig of human hair is a must for formal occasions.

Poor people go barefoot, but you should buy some sandals, which will protect you from scorpions and snakes as well as rocks. You can buy a reed pair from a stand on the edge of the marshes. If you are feeling rich, buy a leather pair from the saddler in the market. They will last longer.

At night, it can get very cold under the clear skies, especially out in the desert. So always carry a linen cape or a woolen shawl with you.

Tattooes

In the market you cannot miss the line for the tattooer. This skilled craftsman uses sharp bronze tools to inject black and blue colors under the skin. But before you join the line for a tattoo of your own, a reminder: in Egypt, tattooes are vulgar and only singers, dancers, musicians, and prostitutes have them.

PERSONAL HYGIENE

Egyptians are very clean and tidy, so you must wash well or you will give offense. There are no bathtubs. Instead, the servants will bring you a jug of water and a bowl so you can wash your body every morning, and clean your hands and face before and after every meal. Rich people get their servants to pour the water over them, sometimes through a sieve to make a shower.

You should also ask for a little salt to rinse out your mouth in the morning. This ritual is known as *sen shem shem*, which means "cleansing of mouth and teeth".

To stop their skin becoming dry in the hot climate, Egyptians rub themselves with greasy ointments made from cat, hippopotamus, or crocodile fat. Women also wear deodorants smelling of dates or frankincense, or exotic oils such as myrrh.

Even your children should wear *kohl*, an eye make-up produced from black minerals. As well as looking good, it keeps away flies, acts as a disinfectant and protects the eyes from bright sunlight. You will also notice that women and priests carry metal tweezers for plucking their eyebrows, and thin blades for cleaning and cutting their nails. Women also color their nails, palms, and the soles of their feet with a yellowy dye made from the leaves of the henna plant.

HEALTH

Like any hot country, Egypt has many dangerous diseases. Malaria, carried by the mosquitoes that breed in the marshes by the river, is one of the worst. The mosquitoes are particularly bad in October and November, as the flood goes down. You can use a repellent made with soda or fresh date oil – spray this in your room to keep the mosquitoes away at night. Smallpox and polio are also problems, so take whatever your medical expert advises and bring extra in case you cannot get them locally.

ACCIDENTS

Wild animals are another cause for concern, especially if you have children. The most dangerous are hippopotamuses and crocodiles, which are everywhere in the river. But snakes are also common and they kill even more people each year. The *asp* or Egyptian cobra is the most dangerous. Scorpions also cause many deaths.

The Egyptians protect their families from these beasts by making offerings to the gods or setting up altars in their houses. If you want to do this too, go to the temple and ask a priest to explain the procedure. You will have to make a small donation to the temple.

WRITING

For foreigners, Egyptian hieroglyphs (picture-writing) are both fascinating and confusing. There are more than 700 different symbols. You will see hieroglyphic inscriptions on statues, monuments, jewelery, and good luck charms everywhere you go. Here are a few clues to help you decipher them.

Every word is written exactly as it sounds, using symbols to represent sounds or whole words. A few symbols are simple pictures, easy to work out – for instance a sun, pronounced "ra," means "day." But most are more abstract shapes, and have different meanings according to the way they are used. Learning the 24 letters of the alphabet is a good start, but you should also look out for other clues to help you understand a text. For example, a crouching man means the subject is a person, while a pair of legs tells you that there is a verb such as "walk" or "run" in the text.

Also pay attention to the way animals or people are facing. If they have been drawn looking to the right, the text is read from left to right; if they face left, it is read the other way. The same text can also be written in columns read from the top or the bottom.

Another thing to look for are *cartouches*, oval loops that contain the name of a pharaoh. Learn to recognize the cartouche of the present pharaoh, plus a few famous names such as Thutmose III and Ramses the Great, then you will be able to date statues, buildings, obelisks, and so on from their inscriptions.

If you really can't make sense of hieroglyphs, remember that most Egyptians cannot read or write either. The only ones who can do so with ease are the scribes, but they spent four or five years at a special school learning to master the language. For them, learning to read and write was a way to have a good career. For letters, official documents, marriage contracts, and stories, they use another script called *hieratic*. This is a simplified version of hieroglyphs and is always read from right to left.

PAPERWORK

Egypt is a very bureaucratic country, and sometimes it seems as if you need a papyrus (the local type of paper made from the reeds that grow at the edge of the Nile and in the marshes) to do anything. If you are caught without the correct documents, you will have to visit the House of Life (*per ankh* in Egyptian), a part of the temple complex. The scribes who work here will draw up any document you need, for a fee. For simple cases, such as a Book of the Dead or a wedding contract, they use standard papyruses, simply adding your name in hieroglyphs in the right places. They will write out more complicated documents, such as official letters, specially for you, but this service will cost more.

Many Houses of Life are attached to a library, the House of Books. You will find all the classics of Egyptian science, religion, and literature there, on papyrus rolls crammed into hollows in the walls. But you will have to befriend a priest to get in: these treasures are very closely guarded.

FOOD AND DRINK

GOING OUT

You will soon get used to bread and onions, served at lunch and dinner throughout Egypt. Most meals are also accompanied by vegetables such as beans, lentils, chick peas, green peas, leeks, olives, radishes, cucumbers, and a type of lettuce. Aniseed, cumin, dill, fennel, marjoram, mustard, thyme, and coriander are all used to add flavor to meals, but pepper is unknown. Dessert is usually fruit, such as figs, palm fruits, pomegranates, dates, plums or watermelons, or sweet pastries (see below).

Egypt is a paradise for vegetarians. Even fish and duck, the most common meats, are not eaten every day. Red meat is rare, and probably beyond your budget. Poor Egyptians only taste it on feast days or at ceremonies such as weddings, when the family will slaughter a cow or a pig. If you are lucky enough to be invited to a banquet, you may taste the best meat of all, game from the hunt. Antelope, gazelle, wild boar, ostrich, or Barbary sheep may all be on the menu. You

could also be offered fish roe, ostrich eggs, or roast wild birds such as cranes, ducks, quails, and geese.

For breakfast or a quick snack, visit the baker, who makes a wonderful variety of breads and cakes. The most common bread is a flat pancake, often filled with lentils, an egg, or vegetables. Other shapes include tall cones, squares, triangles, and half circles. Many are sweetened with honey, dates, sesame seeds, or fruit. On feast days, the baker makes breads in the shape of cows, women, even penises. These are meant as offerings, to be given to the god in the temple.

Egyptians drink beer with most meals. Be warned: it is home brewed, and can be thick with sediment, so use a straw. Wine is also common, though more expensive. The best vintages are made from grapes, but date and palm wines are also on the menu, and can be very good. The children can drink grape or date juice, which is often safer than water.

Egypt has no restaurants as we know them. But you will find food for sale from stalls on every corner. If you are invited to a meal with a poor family, expect to eat squatting around a big table. Use your hands or pieces of bread to scoop the food out of the common bowl. At the end of the meal your host will pour water over your hands to wash them.

In the evening, you can get a drink in one of the town's many beerhouses. These are excellent spots to meet locals, perhaps over a board game such as *senet.* Expect dancing, singing, and storytelling. Egyptians like enjoying themselves, and drunkenness is common. There is no set closing time for the beer-houses, and at festivals the beer will be served until late.

You will hear music everywhere, at food stalls and in beerhouses, at the market and even in the fields, where a boy will often play the flute while the workers are gathering in the harvest.

GIFTS & SOUVENIRS

Jewelery and lucky charms are excellent gifts to take home for friends. You will find wonderful necklaces, bracelets, and rings in the market, many in glittering gold from the Eastern Desert. The desert also provides gemstones such as carnelian and feldspar; others, such as the rich blue lapis lazuli, are imported. Many earrings and necklaces are made from faience or colored glass. Much Egyptian jewelry includes figures of gods or sacred animals, such as scarab beetles, and inscriptions of magic spells. You can also order rings or pendants with your name, or the name of a friend, inscribed in hieroglyphs in a cartouche.

Shabtis – small, mummy-shaped figures made of faience or wood – also make good gifts. They are meant to be buried with a mummy, and contain a spell stating that they will work the fields for their owner in the afterlife. The Egyptians like to be buried with 365 of them, one for each day of the year.

For children, you will find wooden toys carved to look like wild animals. Many have moving parts, such as lions or hippopotamuses with big teeth and mouths that open and close. Also popular are clay models of animals and mummies. Children like to copy their parents by burying these in "tombs" in the sand.

TOILETS

Only the rich (the sort of people who give their guests cones of wax to put on their wigs) have proper toilets: two blocks of stone, separated by a gap with a bucket of sand. The best toilets have wooden seats. But don't be shy if you are caught out in the street. Most Egyptians relieve themselves out of doors, in specially marked corners or by the river. Women and children collect human and animal dung, mix it with straw, and dry it on their roofs. In winter, they will burn it as fuel.

SPORTS

If you enjoy hunting, Egypt is a perfect holiday destination. The desert is home to many wild beasts which can be hunted with bow and arrow or spear from a chariot. Your guide will control the horses while you fire from a high platform at the back. The most popular game animals are gazelles, antelopes, wild bulls, ostriches, and wild sheep. You can go after lions, hyenas, or leopards, but that is dangerous and expensive.

The marshes are home to other game, such as fish, crocodiles, and hippopotamuses. Wild birds are hunted from papyrus rafts, using throwing sticks like heavy boomerangs.

Swimming in the river is popular, especially during the yearly flood. The Egyptians also enjoy ball games, gymnastics, fencing with long sticks, and formation dancing, with girls always dancing with girls and boys with boys.

When you arrive, check if any sports events are coming up. Archery contests and fencing, boxing, and wrestling matches often take place at the palace, to the cheers of a huge crowd, including the pharaoh.

MONEY & SHOPPING

Egypt has no official money, so most buying and selling is done by bartering: swapping different types of goods. Expert shoppers know what things are worth. Most sales are paid in common goods such as wheat and linen. To get a good deal, you should come to Egypt with some items that are rare and highly valued, such as wood, incense, or ivory.

Some goods are given a value in *debens,* equal to a piece of copper weighing about 91 grams. A goat is worth one deben, while a good wooden bed costs 2.5 debens.

TRASH

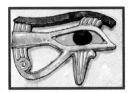

Don't be shy about throwing your trash in the street. It will soon be gobbled up by the town's wild dogs, or hyenas, or vultures that have strayed in from the desert.

FOR THE CHILDREN

Egyptians love children, so yours will be well treated on their holiday. Children play and run wild in the streets, and there is always an adult keeping an eye on them. Your child may want a special Egyptian haircut, the "sidelock of youth," so that he or she looks just like a local child.

One place where Egyptian children are well behaved is at scribe school. An old Egyptian proverb says: "A boy's ears are on his back: he hears when he is beaten."

WHEN TO VISIT

To avoid the heat, the best time to visit Egypt is the winter, from December to February. This corresponds with Peret, the season of sowing and plowing. Unless you are coming for the New Year festival, try to avoid traveling during Akhet, the time of flood. This is the hottest season, and the humidity can be unbearable.

The high waters also make getting about difficult or even impossible. In a year of high floods, many monuments are completely cut off.

Try to come for one of Egypt's festivals. The biggest is the New Year, a five-day holiday to mark the first sighting of Sirius, which the Egyptians call the "Dog Star." This is usually around 19 July. Every town also celebrates the feast day of its god, when the priests carry the statue through the streets and there are masked dancers.

But the very best time to visit is during the *sed* festival, a sort of royal jubilee. This is held every thirty years, to celebrate the pharaoh's rule and show that he is still fit to wear the crown. Spectators from all over the country gather at the palace and cheer as the pharaoh runs a special obstacle course. If he succeeds, and he always does, he is then recrowned in an elaborate ceremony. The celebrations last for weeks, and the whole country comes to a standstill. After this the pharaoh tours the land in his royal barge, greeted by cheering crowds wherever he goes.

GUIDED TOURS

TEMPLE TOUR

Your tour starts in front of the high pylon gateway of the temple, its flags fluttering in the breeze. Follow the large crowd into the massive front courtyard, the only part of the temple open to ordinary people, and join the line waiting to consult the local god. When you reach the front, you will find yourself before a small stone carved with ears and eyes set in a wall. Ask a question, and a voice will answer from within the wall. The local people believe they are talking to the god, though you may think that the speaker is really a priest hidden in a chamber within the wall.

Outside again, take the ferry to the west bank. As you cross the river, look out for a caravan of merchants or desert nomads coming down the cliffs opposite, their heavily loaded donkeys picking their way through the rocks. At the top, the green valley turns abruptly to desert sand. The path on the right leads to the Holy Place, known to foreigners as the Valley of the Kings, where the pharaohs are buried in splendid tombs. Their exact location is a secret, and access is strictly forbidden, though you may be able to pay a craftworker to take you on a tour.

If you can't organize this, be sure to visit the mortuary temple at the foot of the path. Before entering, buy an offering from the priests at the gate. A cone-shaped loaf of bread is popular, though you may want to pay a scribe to write out a wish for you. At some temples you can even buy mummified animals, such as cats or scarab beetles, as offerings. Enter the temple with your offering. Go through the entrance into the pillared courtyard. Then do what every one else does: place your gift before the sacred shrine and say a quiet prayer.

Before you leave, look at the carvings on the walls. These feature hunting scenes, military victories, and the pharaoh kneeling before the gods. Try to decipher the hieroglyphic inscriptions and find the cartouche of the pharaoh who had the temple built. On your way out, look at the obelisks and the huge statues of the pharaoh on either side of the entrance. As the ferryman rows you back across the Nile, it's worth remembering that a large temple employs several thousand people working full-time – just to keep alive the memory of one dead god-king.

BOAT TRIP

A leisurely cruise on the Nile will give you a new view of the town. You can hire a wooden pleasure boat at the quayside. Make sure the captain puts up a sun canopy – it can be very hot out on the river.

The crew will probably start by raising the mast and sailing upstream against the current. Notice all the working ships heading both ways, the crews sweating at the oars or ropes. The barges loaded with high-quality stone for building or carving statues come all the way from Aswan, near the Nubian border to the south. They are heavy, low in the water, and difficult to steer.

You may be surprised by the size and speed of the river. In the narrow valley where the town lies, it is deep and fast-moving. Farther north, in the lush delta, it splits into many wide streams.

The small rafts you see in the shallows belong to local fishermen or couples out for a quiet cruise. Made from bundles of papyrus reeds tied together, they are maneuvred with a long pole.

You will see many peasants down by the river. The farmers may be using wooden machines called *shadufs* to raise water into their irrigation channels. You will see children swimming and women filling large pots with water and loading them onto donkeys. But notice that men are the only ones washing clothes and hanging them up to dry. This is because there are so many crocodiles about that doing the washing is always dangerous.

You will also pass teams of workmen making mud bricks. They mix the red mud from the bank with straw and sand, squash it into wooden molds, turn out the bricks and leave them to dry in the sun. In two or three days, they will be as hard as rock.

As you sail back to the quay, watch the way the pilot uses a heavy weight on a cord to test the water's depth while the captain steers with a large oar mounted at the stern. The sandbanks are always shifting, and boats need flat bottoms to cross them. If you do run aground, hop out and help push the boat clear. But do remember to look out for hippopotamuses and crocodiles before you leap!

VISITING THE PYRAMIDS

No visit to Egypt is complete without a visit to the pyramids. These massive mountains of stone are on the west bank of the Nile at Giza, near the old capital city of Memphis (on the outskirts of modern Cairo). The pyramids are tombs built at the very dawn of Egypt's history, by the great pharaohs of the Old Kingdom (2682 to 2181 BC).

The best way to reach them is, again, by boat. You will land by the massive temple of the pharaoh Khafra. This is worth a visit, if only to see the 23 life-size statues of the pharaoh. Note the falcon god Horus, a sign of royalty, that wraps its wings around the pharaoh's neck.

From this temple, go to the mortuary temple in the shadow of Khafra's pyramid. On your right is the Great Sphinx, carved from a rocky outcrop 188 feet (about 57 meters) long and 66 feet (20 meters) high. It has the body of a crouching lion and the head of a pharaoh, probably Khafra himself. The Egyptians believe that it guards his pyramid.

Just north of Khafra's pyramid is the Great Pyramid.

The first and largest pyramid, it was built in 2550 BC for the pharaoh Khufu. It is huge. Each of the four sides is 759 feet (230 meters) long, and rises to a glittering peak 485 feet (about 147 meters) high. It is said to contain 2,300,000 blocks of stone, the biggest weighing ten tons each. Inside, a network of passages leads to the pharaoh's burial chamber. The pyramid's sides are covered in fine limestone, polished white and gleaming in the sun. In front of it stand three smaller tombs, called the queens' pyramids because they are believed to have held the bodies of Khufu's favorite wives. Unfortunately, like all the Giza pyramids, their treasures were stolen long ago, in the period of chaos that followed the end of the Old Kingdom.

To the south of the Giza complex is the smaller pyramid of Menkaura, who may have been Khafra's son. He also built three queens' pyramids.

How were the pyramids built? Not by slaves, but by workers who wanted to help their pharaoh achieve eternal life. During the flood, when work in the fields stopped, as many as 100,000 men dragged blocks of stone up ramps to the top of the pyramid. Even with this great labor force, it took twenty years to complete Khufu's Great Pyramid.

 # GLOSSARY

Amulet Lucky charm. Ancient Egyptians wore amulets to ward off evil. They also placed them in the wrappings of mummies.

Amun-Ra The sun god and Egypt's most important god during the New Kingdom. He had a mysterious nature – "Amun" means "hidden" in Egyptian. His temple, at Karnak, was the largest and most powerful in Egypt. The ruins are in the modern town of Luxor.

Book of the Dead Collection of more than 200 magic spells. They were designed to help a dead person's soul on the dangerous journey through the underworld. The "book" was usually a long scroll of papyrus, with many illustrations.

Canopic jars Containers that held the four vital organs — liver, lungs, stomach, and intestines — of a dead person. They were placed in the tomb next to his or her mummy.

Delta Flat, marshy area where a river meets the sea. The Nile delta is very lush. The vineyards there provided the pharaohs with their finest wines.

Ebony Valuable, extremely hard black wood. The Egyptians imported it from Africa to the south of their country and used it to make beautiful furniture and luxuries such as make-up boxes.

Faience Type of glazed pottery. It was often blue or green.

Incense Substance that is burned for its pleasant smell. Egyptian priests burned incense to purify the air and please the temple's god.

Ivory Tusks and teeth of elephants, hippopotamuses, or walruses. Egyptian artists used it for carvings and furniture inlay.

Lotus Waterlily that grew on the Nile River. Lotuses were often shown in tomb paintings.

Mummy Preserved body, usually wrapped in linen bandages. The Egyptians mummified their bodies to be sure that they would be born again in the next world.

Nubia Egypt's southern neighbor, an ancient land now split between Egypt and the Sudan. It was part of Egypt's kingdom for many centuries. Nubian pharaohs even ruled Egypt from 747 to 656 BC.

Osiris God of death and rebirth. According to legend, he was a king killed by his evil brother, Seth. His wife, Isis, put his body back together, to make the first mummy, and Osiris was reborn as a god.

Papyrus Reed that grew by the banks of the Nile. The Egyptians made a papery writing material from its stem. They also made boats by tying together bundles of papyrus reeds.

Pharaoh Egyptian king. The word means "The Great House" in Egyptian, and first referred to the king's palace. Traditionally, the pharaoh was a man, but a woman could rule. The most famous woman pharaoh is Hatshepsut, who ruled from 1479 to 1457 BC.

Punt A land visited by Egyptian traders. Experts are still not sure of its exact location, but it was probably on the east African coast in modern Somalia. A painting of the Queen of Punt from 1450 BC suggests that she suffered from a severe muscular disease.

Pylon Massive gateway to an Egyptian temple.

Scribe Professional writer. The majority of Egyptians could not read or write, so the scribe had an important place in Egyptian society. Most officials were trained as scribes.

INDEX